Blessed are the dead who die in the Lord

© Roger Carswell 2003

ISBN 1 85792 894 6

Published in 2003 by
Christian Focus Publications, Geanies House,
Fearn, Ross-shire, IV20 ITW, Scotland

www.christianfocus.com

Cover design by Alister MacInnes

Printed and bound by
Bell & Bain, Glasgow

Blessed are the dead who die in the Lord
By Roger Carswell

The Book of Revelation graphically and dramatically describes events surrounding the Second Coming of our Lord Jesus Christ. At one stage John, the author, describes an interruption of seven angels who are sent to explain what is happening. One of these seven says,

> 'Blessed are the dead who die in the Lord, from now on'
> (Revelation 14 v 13).

God, the Holy Spirit, reinforces this with the words:

> 'Yes, they will rest from their labours, for their deeds will follow them' (Revelation 14 v 13).

So the New Testament which begins with Jesus' Beatitudes, ends with Beatitudes and Blessings for God's people. And although the words were written for those who die in the

Great Tribulation, they have been an assurance that has encouraged all God's people who have stared death in the face. There are thousands of examples one could quote, but here is one. Donald Cargill, the Scottish Covenanter spoke his last words before being executed on the 27th July, 1681:

> "The Lord knows, I go up this ladder in less fear and perturbed of mind than ever I entered the pulpit to preach... Farewell, all relations and friends in Christ; farewell all acquaintances and all earthly enjoyments; farewell reading and preaching, praying and believing, wanderings, reproaches and sufferings. Welcome joy unspeakable and full of glory. Welcome Father, Son and Holy Ghost. Into thy hands I commit my spirit."

Death is an enemy. It is a great destroyer. In a foul swoop death takes all the aspirations of a person, the dreams of their heart and the memories of the mind. Death severs the ties that bind a person to their loved ones. Death's work is relentless, cruel and merciless. Yet God's verdict concerning His children who die in the Lord is that they are blessed of the Lord.

How then, can that be? It is because of:

Where they are

Those who die in the Lord are in heaven. The Creator who made the majestic snow-capped peaks of the Alps, the rushing mountain streams, the brilliantly coloured autumn leaves, the carpets of wildflowers, the glistening fins of the fish and graceful gliding of the swan, as well as the lilting notes of a canary's song and shimmer of a dew drop in the early morning, is the same Creator who has prepared our heavenly home. More than that, the Lord Himself is the centre of heaven; to be there is to be in His presence.

Heaven is a place of no pain, hospitals, and grief. There are no broken hearts, homes, lives or dreams. There is no mental retardation, muscular dystrophy, Parkinson's disease, cancer, multiple sclerosis, blindness, lameness or deafness. There are no fires, floods, sickness, death or war.
The Bible puts it like this:

> "And I heard a loud voice from heaven say, 'Behold the tabernacle of God is with men, and He will dwell with them, and they shall be His people, and God Himself will be with them and be their God. And God will wipe away

every tear from their eyes; there shall be no more death, no sorrow, nor crying, and there shall be no more pain, for the former things have passed away'.

Then He who sat on the throne said,

'Behold, I will make all things new'.

And He said to me,

'Write, for these words are true and faithful'" (Revelation 21 v 3-4).

Like a bird out of its cage, we shall be liberated from the drag of this mortal life.

Who they are with

"Absent from the body is to be present
with the Lord" (2 Corinthians 5 v 8).

The Lord is the One who stood to welcome the first Christian martyr, Stephen. He will welcome safe home each of His children who have passed through the valley of the shadow of death.

All God's people will be in heaven. Just imagine a place where all the saints of all time will be with the Lord Jesus, enjoying Him and unspoiled fellowship with each other. There is an illustration of this in John 12. When Jesus raised Jairus' daughter back to life, she sat up, opened her eyes and saw Jesus first. Then, no doubt she would have seen her father and mother, and then Peter, James and John.

First, the Saviour, then her loved ones, then the other followers of Jesus –

*isn't that how we will see
each other in heaven?*

7

What they are doing

The Bible describes the citizens of heaven as

praising and worshipping God.

The rest, which is to be enjoyed, is not that of sitting on a cloud, but rather that of a sailor home from the seas, or a solider home from the battle. They will work without weariness, and have responsibility with restoration. The immediate presence of Christ will be heaven for us.

Jesus is never bored, and nor will be
His children who are in His presence!

How long is it for?

Heaven is everlasting and eternal, which tells us of the quantity and quality of this home. At the moment of death, those who have trusted Christ are immediately received into the presence of the Lord.

> Sleep after toil; port after stormy seas;
> ease after war, life after death."

Why they are there

Sadly, it is possible to die with unforgiven sin, without God, without Christ, and without hope. Jesus tenderly warned about hell for those who do not receive the pardon, which He purchased on the cross. Jesus took the sting of death, which is sin, on Himself on the cross. Christ carried the can for all our wrongdoing. He died so that all that cuts us off from God, and would condemn us forever, might be forgiven. Jesus conquered the conqueror death, by rising again from the dead. He has ascended to heaven and will one day return in glory, as Lord, King and Judge.

Our eternal destiny is not decided by the words of the parson at the funeral. And if a person does not believe in judgement, it does not alter the fact that every individual will stand before God as the judge. Those who are in heaven are there not through works of righteousness that they have done, but because of God's mercy in which they have trusted.

Does the world say,

"Blessed are the living?"
God says, "Blessed are the dead, who die in the Lord."

The 18th century Bible commentator, Matthew Henry,

expressed his confidence in words that he hoped would be read after his death by anyone who might unduly mourn his passing. He wrote:

> "Would you like to know where I am? I am at home in my Father's house, in the mansions prepared for me here. I am where I want to be – no longer on the stormy sea, but in God's safe, quiet harbour. My sowing time is done, and I am reaping; my joy is as the joy of harvest. Would you like to know how it is with me? I am made perfect in holiness. Grace is swallowed up in glory. Would you like to know what I am doing? I see God, not as through a glass darkly, but face to face. I am engaged in the sweet enjoyment of my precious Redeemer. I am singing hallelujahs to Him who sits upon the throne, and I am constantly praising Him. Would you know what blessed company I keep? It is better than the best on earth. Here are the holy angels and the spirits of just men made perfect... I am with many of my old acquaintances with whom I worked and prayed, and who have come here before me. Lastly, would you know how long this will continue? It is a dawn that never fades! After millions and millions of ages, it will be as fresh as it is now. Therefore, weep not for me!"

In times of sorrow, it is good to know that God, who made heaven and earth, has spoken to all humanity through His word, the Bible.

> *As we open it and read it, we are*
> *in effect opening the lips of God*
> *and allowing Him to speak to us.*

Conclusion

I would recommend systematically reading a chapter or so of the Bible day by day. Perhaps you could start with the Gospel of John. You will see how Jesus deals with the issue of suffering and death particularly in chapters 11 and 21. You will read how He teaches by His own life and example what life is all about, and how we can know a close friendship with God. As with any other book, though, I recommend starting at the beginning of John's Gospel and reading through to the end. As you read, ask God to reveal Himself to you.

However, I have selected from various parts of the Bible, passages which I trust will be of help at this difficult time.

Romans 8 v 31-39

What then shall we say to these things? If God is for us, who can be against us? He who did not spare His own Son, but delivered Him up for us all, how shall He not with Him also freely give us all things? Who shall bring a charge against God's elect? It is God who justifies.

Who is he who condemns? It is Christ who died,

and furthermore is also risen, who is even at the right hand of God, who also makes intercession for us. Who shall separate us from the love of Christ? Shall tribulation, or distress, or persecution, or famine, or nakedness, or peril, or sword? As it is written: "For Your sake we are killed all day long; we are accounted as sheep for the slaughter." Yet in all these things we are more than conquerors through Him who loved us. For I am persuaded that neither death nor life, nor angels nor principalities nor powers, nor things present nor things to come, nor height nor depth, nor any other created thing, shall be able to separate us from the love of God which is in Christ Jesus our Lord.

2 Corinthians 1 v 3-7

Blessed be the God and Father of our Lord Jesus Christ, the Father of mercies and God of all comfort, who comforts us in all our tribulation, that we may be able to comfort those who are in any trouble, with the comfort with which we ourselves are comforted by God. For as the sufferings of Christ abound in us, so our consolation also abounds through Christ.

Now if we are afflicted, it is for your consolation and salvation, which is effective for enduring the same sufferings which we also suffer. Or if we are comforted, it is for your consolation and salvation. And our hope for you is steadfast, because we know that as you are partakers of the sufferings, so also you will partake of the consolation.

Psalm 11 v 1-7

In the LORD I put my trust; how can you say to my soul, "Flee as a bird to your mountain"?

For look! The wicked bend their bow, they make ready their arrow on the string, that they may shoot secretly at the upright in heart. If the foundations are destroyed, what can the righteous do? The LORD is in His holy temple, the LORD'S throne is in heaven; his eyes behold, his eyelids test the sons of men. The LORD tests the righteous, but the wicked and the one who loves violence His soul hates. Upon the wicked He will rain coals, fire and brimstone and a burning wind shall be the portion of their cup. For the LORD is righteous, he loves righteousness; his countenance beholds the upright.

Psalm 38 v 9-11, 21-22

Lord, all my desire is before You; and my sighing is not hidden from You. My heart pants, my strength fails me; as for the light of my eyes, it also has gone from me. My loved ones and my friends stand aloof from my plague, and my relatives stand afar off.

Do not forsake me, O LORD; O my God, be not far from me! Make haste to help me, O Lord, my salvation!

Psalm 31 v 9-12, 14

Have mercy on me, O LORD, for I am in trouble; my eye wastes away with grief, yes, my soul and my body! For my life is spent with grief, and my years with sighing;

my strength fails because of my iniquity, and my bones waste away.

I am a reproach among all my enemies, but especially among my neighbours, and am repulsive to my acquaintances; those who see me outside flee from me. I am forgotten like a dead man, out of mind; I am like a broken vessel.

But as for me, I trust in You, O LORD; I say, "You are my God."

John 14 v 1-6 and 18-23 and 25-27

"Let not your heart be troubled; you believe in God, believe also in Me. "In My Father's house are many mansions; if it were not so, I would have told you. I go to prepare a place for you. "And if I go and prepare a place for you, I will come again and receive you to Myself; that where I am, there you may be also. "And where I go you know, and the way you know."

Thomas said to Him, "Lord, we do not know where You are going, and how can we know the way?" Jesus said to him, "I am the way, the truth, and the life. No one comes to the Father except through Me.

"I will not leave you orphans; I will come to you. A little while longer and the world will see Me no more, but you will see Me. Because I live, you will live also. At that day you will know that I am in My Father, and you in Me, and I in you. He who has My commandments and keeps them, it is he who loves Me. And he who loves Me will be loved by My Father, and I will love him and manifest Myself to him." Judas (not Iscariot) said to Him, "Lord, how is it that You will manifest Yourself to us, and not to the world?" Jesus answered and said to him, "If anyone loves Me, he will keep My word; and My Father will love him, and We will come to him and make Our home with him.

"These things I have spoken to you while being present with you. But the Helper, the Holy Spirit, whom the Father will send in My name, He will teach you all things, and bring to your remembrance all things that I said to you. "Peace I leave with you, My peace I give to you; not as the world gives do I give to you. Let not your heart be troubled, neither let it be afraid."

1 Corinthians 15 v 50-57

Now this I say, brethren, that flesh and blood cannot inherit the kingdom of God; nor does corruption inherit incorruption. Behold, I tell you a mystery: We shall not all sleep, but we shall all be changed - in a moment, in the twinkling of an eye, at the last trumpet. For the trumpet will sound, and the dead will be raised incorruptible, and we shall be changed. For this corruptible must put on incorruption, and this mortal must put on immortality. So when this corruptible has put on incorruption, and this mortal has put on immortality, then shall be brought to pass the saying that is written: "Death is swallowed up in victory." "O Death, where is your sting? O Hades, where is your victory?" The sting of death is sin, and the strength of sin is the law. But thanks be to God, who gives us the victory through our Lord Jesus Christ.

Isaiah 25 v 6-10

And in this mountain the LORD of hosts will make for all people a feast of choice pieces, a feast of wines on the lees, of fat things full of marrow, of well-refined wines on the lees.

And He will destroy on this mountain the surface of the covering cast over all people, and the veil that is spread over all nations. He will swallow up death forever, and the Lord GOD will wipe away tears from all faces; the rebuke of His people he will take away from all the earth; for the LORD has spoken. And it will be said in that day: "Behold, this is our God; we have waited for Him, and He will save us. This is the LORD; we have waited for Him; we will be glad and rejoice in His salvation." For on this mountain the hand of the LORD will rest, and Moab shall be trampled down under Him, as straw is trampled.

Revelation 21 v 1-7

Now I saw a new heaven and a new earth, for the first heaven and the first earth had passed away. Also there was no more sea. Then I, John, saw the holy city, New Jerusalem, coming down out of heaven from God, prepared as a bride adorned for her husband. And I heard a loud voice from heaven saying, "Behold, the tabernacle of God is with men, and He will dwell with them, and they shall be His people. God Himself will be with them and be their God.

"And God will wipe away every tear from their eyes; there shall be no more death, nor sorrow, nor crying. There shall be no more pain, for the former things have passed away." Then He who sat on the throne said, "Behold, I make all things new." And He said to me, "Write, for these words are true and faithful." And He said to me, "It is done! I am the Alpha and the Omega, the Beginning and the End. I will give of the fountain of the water of life freely to him who thirsts. He who overcomes shall inherit all things, and I will be his God and he shall be My son."

Also by Roger Carswell

Comfort in times of Sorrow

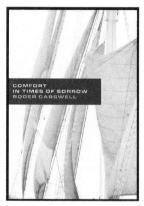

A sailing ship spreads her white sails to the morning breeze as she sets sail for the ocean. She looks beautiful and strong. You watch the ship until it seems like a speck of white cloud just where the sea and sky meet each other. Someone next to you says, "There, she's gone."

But has she gone? She is just as large in mast and hull as she was when she left the shore. Just at the moment when someone says, "She's gone" another voice on a distant shore shouts, "She's here!".

Death is similar. Earth's loss is eternity's gain. Each one of us has an endless existence, first in this world, and then in the next.

May you be comforted in your grief with these words of encouragement.

ISBN 1 85792 8954